MOGGICHAT'S ADVENTURES

Carolyn Helena Silberfeld

Acknowledgements

My grateful thanks must go to our adorable Moggichat and my wonderful husband, Robert (Boo), who has been unwavering in his love, support and encouragement to write this story. I would also like to thank my lovely cousin Heath Lynn for her editorial advice. None of this could have been possible without the exceptional illustrations, by Dave Roger, which brought our beautiful Moggichat to life.

A Cat Without a Home

Moggichat was an adventurous black cat,
but he was also a sad cat because he did not have a
home, and he was always hungry.

At the beginning of the summer, while exploring,
he discovered a huge garden.
He found a good hiding place in the bushes
where he could watch people coming
and going from the big house.
He felt safe there.

One day, two people called Bunny and Boo saw something moving in the bushes.
"Did you see that?" Bunny whispered, peering closer. "Something's definitely in there," Boo replied, "too small to be a fox...maybe a stray cat?"

Moggichat backed deeper into his hiding place.
But the people seemed friendly.
"Poor thing," Bunny said softly.
"Let's leave some food out and see what happens."

They started leaving food for him in a tray on the terrace. When they went indoors Moggichat cautiously came out of his hiding place and ate up all the food.

This happened every day until one day he found his food not in a tray but in a very smart bowl!

It had a picture of a cat and a name on it, but Moggichat did not know what it said because he could not read.

He liked the food and waited each day for his bowl to arrive. After a few more days, Bunny and Boo came on to the terrace and watched Moggichat.
He saw them and was very frightened, but carried on eating because he was so hungry.

Slowly, Moggichat let Bunny and Boo come closer to him.
He was nervous but happy.

The Little Warm House

Next, they bought Moggichat a little house because it was getting cold. He was not sure what to do with the house, so he walked around it, sniffing and sniffing to check it out.

The next day he saw a small bowl of cat treats in the new house. He went in to eat them and found a very comfortable thermal blanket on the floor of the house that would keep him warm at night.

When winter came, he began coming inside the big house and eating there too. Then he started sleeping in the lovely warm house during the day. It had plenty of comfortable places to sleep, and Boo and Bunny gave him more food during the day.

At the end of each day, he went outside to have more adventures in the garden and beyond. When it was cold he slept in his little house in the garden.
He did this every day until spring arrived.

Lost and Found

One breezy spring morning Moggichat got lost.
He could not find his way home.
He was very frightened.

He was ill too, which made things even worse.

After a week he crawled home. When Bunny and Boo saw him, they took him to the vet straight away. Chloe the vet was very kind to Moggichat, and he liked her too.

Moggichat had a very high temperature and had to stay at the vet for four days. He missed Bunny and Boo very much. He thought they were going to leave him there and became very sad.

Chloe told Bunny and Boo that Moggichat would get better, but because he could become ill again if he went outside, he needed to stay in the house.

Indoor Adventures

Moggichat was so happy when Bunny and Boo came to get him from the vet that he ran into the box they had brought to carry him home.

Moggichat found it hard to stay in the house at first but then he realised what fun he could have. The house was big with many interesting corners. There were also lots of spiders, which Moggichat loved to catch.

When Moggichat lived outside he used to stretch to scratch all the big trees in the garden. When he had to stay indoors, he started to scratch the carpet. So, Bunny and Boo bought him a large scratching post for the kitchen and four smaller ones for the places he liked to be. There was one in the living room, one in the study, one on the landing, and one in the hall.

Sometimes he was a bit naughty,
He scratched all the chairs he sat on.
Bunny and Boo were not happy about that.

Sometimes he did it to get their attention.
He loved being with them and
especially liked Bunny's chairs in all the rooms

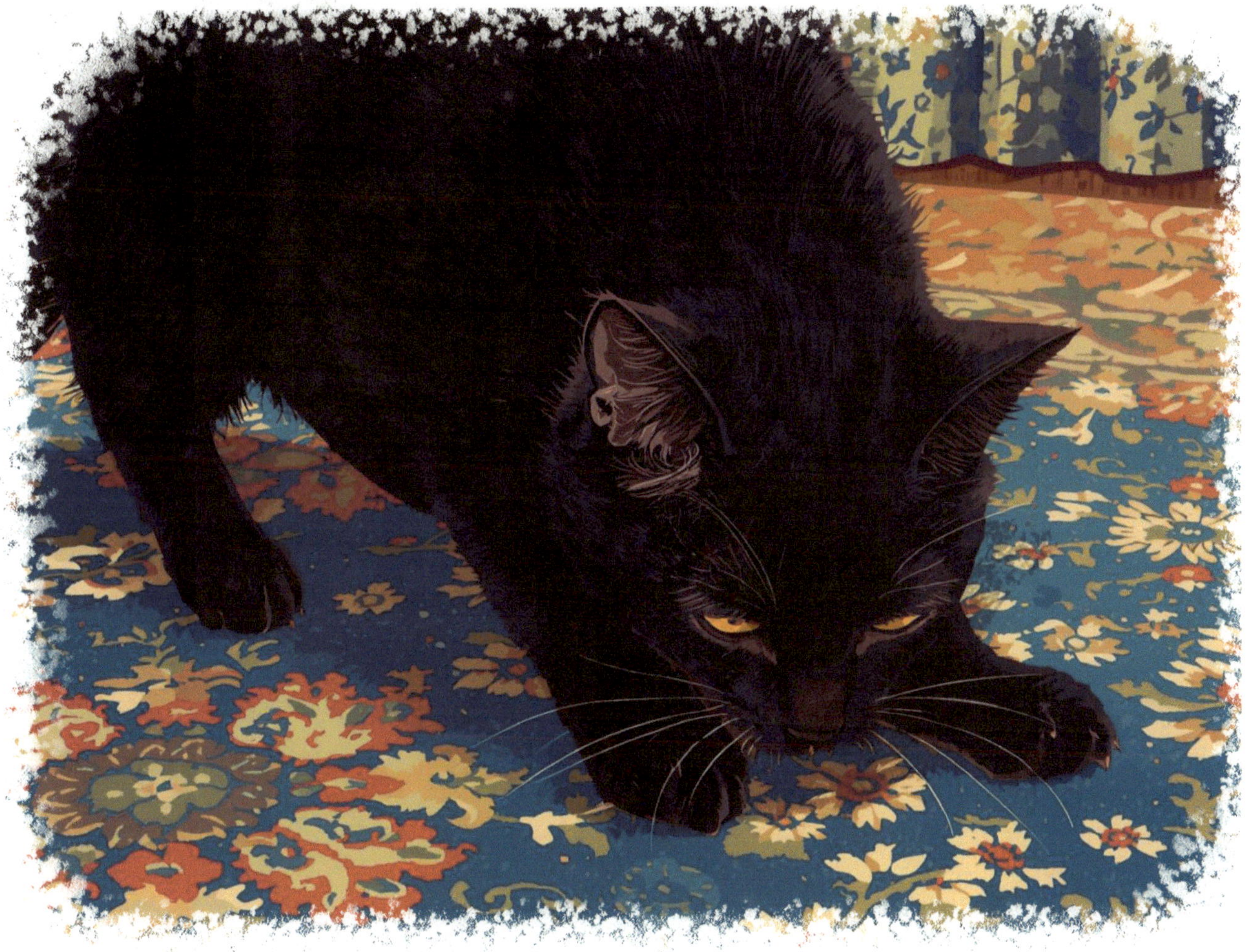

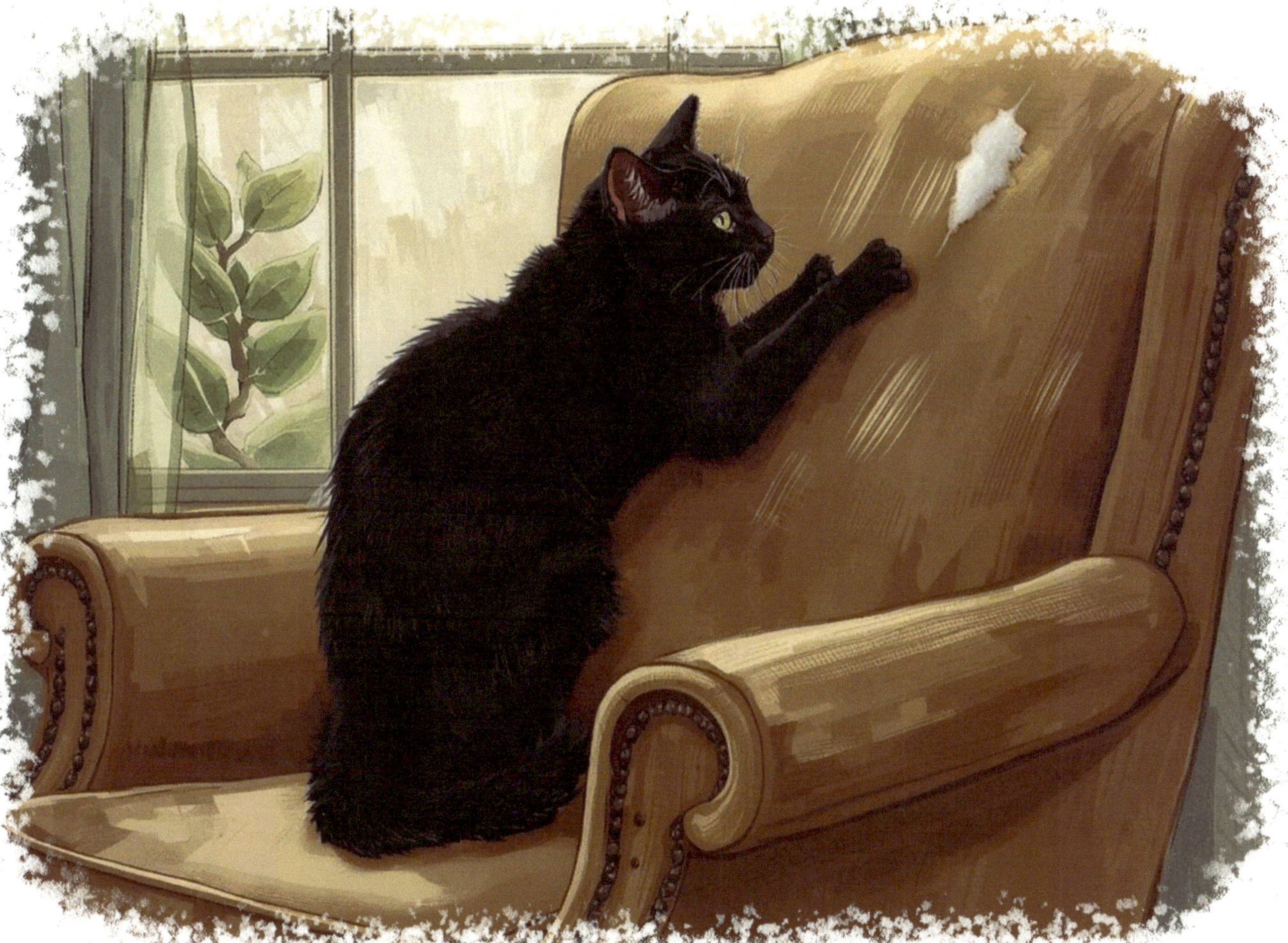

A Cat's Kingdom

Bunny and Boo bought Moggichat two beds — one large and one small - and a very soft rug as well as four blankets to put on the chairs that Moggichat liked to scratch.

At night Moggichat slept downstairs. He always knew it was bedtime when he heard the rustle of the treats packet. He came running from wherever he was to eat his favourite treats from the hands of either Bunny or Boo.

Sometimes he sat on the kitchen shelf, watching the movement of other animals outside in the garden until he was tired enough to go to sleep.

In spite of having two beds, a comfortable rug, and four very cosy blankets, Moggichat preferred to sleep on the chairs that did not have blankets on them.

Every morning Boo went downstairs and gave Moggichat lots of cuddles. After this Moggichat ran into the kitchen for his food. He liked food with lots of gravy and he loved cat treats. He also liked to lick the lid of the empty pot of yoghurt when Boo made breakfast for Bunny and himself. Moggichat was a very happy cat.

Playtime and Mischief

When Moggichat was feeling much better, he ran around very fast — up and down the stairs and into all the rooms.

He liked jumping on beds but he always waited outside the bedroom in the morning as Bunny did not like him sneaking in and bouncing on her bed.

Sometimes he followed her around. Other times he stood outside the cupboard where his food was kept to show he wanted more.

He soon began sitting beside the dining room table while Bunny and Boo ate looking as though he wanted to try their food.

Eventually, Bunny and Boo let him lick little tastes of different things from their fingers. He was such a clever cat, knowing exactly when meals were being prepared and served.

A Gourmet Cat

Moggichat tried lots of foods on his new small mat on the floor by the dining room table, though he still liked eating food from the hands and fingers of Bunny and Boo. Yogurt, hummus, avocado, cheese, cream cheese, and ham proved to be his favourites.

He also had his own three bowls in the sunroom — one for wet food, like cat food in gravy and cat soup, one for water, and one for dried snacks. Once a day he was given snacks to help keep his teeth clean.

Boo and Moggichat played together for hours. Boo got Moggichat a toy mouse on a stretchy string. The mouse squeaked every time it was touched. In response, Moggichat would run up and down the stairs, balancing on the bannisters. Bunny and Boo were frightened that he would fall off and tumble to the floor below, but somehow he always stayed on.

Back to the Garden

Moggichat longed to go outside again.
He would sit by the sliding door in the sunroom,
hoping that he could go out.
Bunny and Boo were afraid to let Moggichat outside
in case he became ill or got lost again.
They also did not want him to be run over by a car
like Millie, a neighbour's cat.

Bunny and Boo decided to get a harness for Moggichat so that he could go for walks in the large garden. At first he refused to have the harness put on him and ran away whenever he saw it. Gradually he realised he could explore if he wore the harness, so he let Bunny and Boo put it on him.

Everything was fine until one day Moggichat pulled the long lead very hard and slipped out of the harness. Bunny and Boo were very worried, but Moggichat did not go far and let them pick him up and take him back inside.

Boo and Bunny knew that Moggichat did not like the harness, so as time went by Moggichat went into the garden with Boo and Bunny without the harness.

He liked going into the garden with Bunny when she was hanging up the washing.

He liked going outside with Boo when he was doing the gardening or in the greenhouse.

Happy at Last

Bunny and Boo loved Moggichat, and he loved them right back. After each day's excitement, he would curl up beside them and rest. He never gave up on his adventures. He still chased butterflies, climbed furniture, and explored every corner. But now, he always returned to a place that was warm, safe, and his. A place he never had before: a home.

www.ingramcontent.com/pod-product-compliance
Lightning Source LLC
Chambersburg PA
CBHW041508220426
43661CB00017B/1281